PIANO SOLO / PIANO • VOCAL • CHORDS

JIM BRICKMAN
HOME

Alfred

Produced by
Alfred Music Publishing Co., Inc.
P.O. Box 10003
Van Nuys, CA 91410-0003
alfred.com

Printed in USA.

ISBN-10: 0-7390-7592-6
ISBN-13: 978-0-7390-7592-0

Album Artwork: © 2010 Somerset Entertainment Ltd.

CONTENTS

THANK YOU

Words and Music by
JIM BRICKMAN and VICTORIA SHAW

Thank You - 5 - 1

SWEET REUNION

Composed by
JIM BRICKMAN

Slowly ♩ = 72

(with pedal)

10

THROUGH THE YEARS

Composed by
JIM BRICKMAN

14

COUNTRY ROAD

Composed by
JIM BRICKMAN

Slowly ♩ = 52

(with pedal)

Country Road - 4 - 2

Country Road - 4 - 4

LOST & FOUND

Composed by
JIM BRICKMAN

Moderately slow ♩ = 76

(with pedal)

Lost & Found - 4 - 1

Lost & Found - 4 - 2

A WINTER'S NIGHT

Composed by
JIM BRICKMAN

Slowly, with motion ♩ = 60

A Winter's Night - 3 - 1

SUNSHINE

Composed by
JIM BRICKMAN

Sunshine - 5 - 1

BEDTIME STORY

Composed by
JIM BRICKMAN

Slowly ♩. = 52

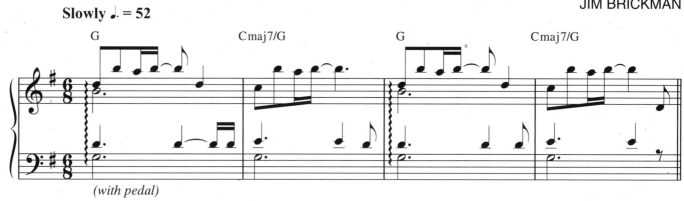

(with pedal)

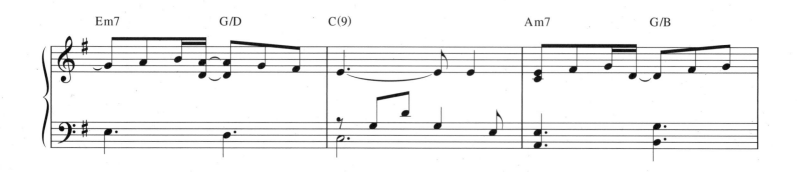

Bedtime Story - 7 - 1

34

38

Bedtime Story - 7 - 7

SANCTUARY

Composed by
JIM BRICKMAN

Slowly, with expression ($\quarternote$ = 72)

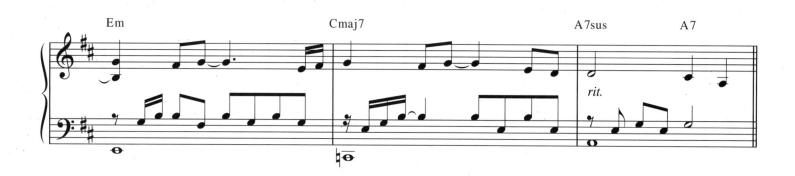

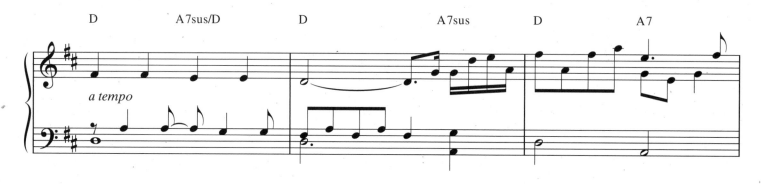

41

Sanctuary - 3 - 3

BY THE FIRE

Composed by
JIM BRICKMAN

3:10

Moderately ♩ = 120

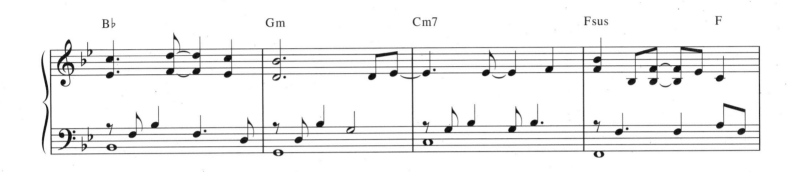

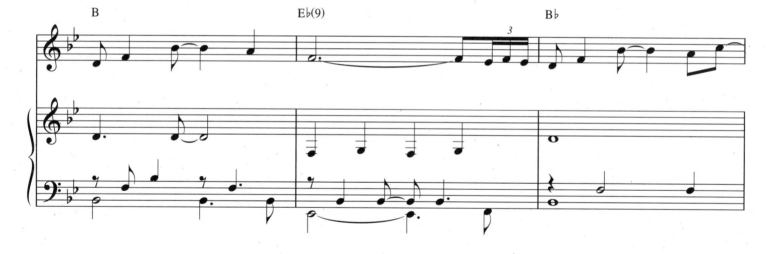

By the Fire - 6 - 4

46

By the Fire - 6 - 5

By the Fire - 6 - 6

HIDEAWAY

Composed by
JIM BRICKMAN

50

Hideaway - 4 - 3

SUNDAY DRIVE

Composed by
JIM BRICKMAN

54

RIVERBEND

Composed by
JIM BRICKMAN

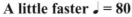

Riverbend - 4 - 1

SUMMER DAYS

Composed by
JIM BRICKMAN

Moderately slow, with movement ♩ = 80

Summer Days - 5 - 1

62

64

Summer Days - 5 - 5

TRADITIONS

Composed by
JIM BRICKMAN

Moderately ♩ = 60

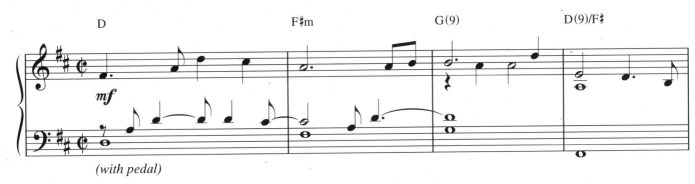

(with pedal)

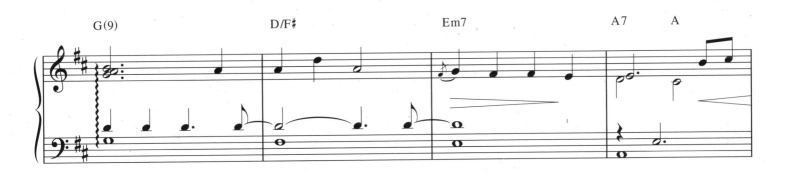

Traditions - 5 - 1

66

WELCOME HOME

Words and Music by
JIM BRICKMAN and VICTORIA SHAW

Welcome Home - 5 - 1

72

Chorus:

home, wel - come home._____ I've_ been pray-ing for this day___ since you've_ been___

___ gone._____ Wel-come back_____ to___ these_ arms that have been wait-ing for you__ for so__

___ long._____ Wel - come home._____ Wel-

dim.

come home.___ *rit.* *freely* *8va*

WHAT WE BELIEVE IN

Words and Music by
JIM BRICKMAN and TOM DOUGLAS

1. Fun-ny, just the oth-er day, I was walk-ing down the street.

What We Believe In - 7 - 1

78

80

Fm7　　　　　　　Ab/Eb　　　　　　　　Db(9)

love　　is worth　the　pain_____　　and　all　the tears___　you

Bbsus　　　　　Eb　Eb/G　　Ab(9)　　Bb7sus

cry._____

cresc.　　　f

Eb　Cm7　Ab(9)　　Bb7sus Bb7　Eb　　Eb/G

Oh,_____　and　if　see - ing is___　be -

Ab(9)　Bb7sus　Cm7　　　　　F7sus　F

liev - ing,___　　I look in-to___ the sky,___　　and there　you are.___　You're

What We Believe In - 7 - 6

BREATHE, DREAM, PRAY, LOVE

Words and Music by
JIM BRICKMAN, VICTORIA SHAW, AMY SKY
and JOCHEM VAN DER SAAG

Slowly ♩ = 80

*Original recording in F# major.

Breathe, Dream, Pray, Love - 7 - 1